THE
COTSWOLDS
from the air

DAVID GODDARD
Text by
JOHN MANNION

MYRIAD
LONDON

First published in 2011 by Myriad Books Limited, 35 Bishopsthorpe Road, London SE26 4PA

Photographs copyright © 2011 David Goddard Text copyright © 2011 John Mannion

ISBN 1 84746 383 5
EAN 978 1 84746 383 8

Designed by Jerry Goldie Graphic Design

Printed in China

www.myriadbooks.com

Previous page: Winchcombe, near Gloucester, with Sudeley Castle in the foreground.

INTRODUCTION

I have been an aerial photographer for 16 years, operating out of Blackbushe Airport, south of Reading. I often fly west along the M4 corridor to the southern Cotswolds with my pilot. As we start our journey, we usually witness an eclectic mix of architecture, which often lacks any sense of harmony. But in an aircraft, things change quickly. As we cross the Lambourn Downs threading between Faringdon and Highworth, the sense of a new landscape starts to appear; here is a different and distinct part of England that's all too readily identifiable even from the air. It's not just the green rolling countryside that gives the Cotswolds its true identity but the area's distinctive honey-coloured villages and towns.

As you continue north-west, even in an aircraft, you can almost feel the lush grass terrain of the central and north Cotswolds rise up slowly into the majestic rolling downland which forms the perfect backdrop to such villages and towns as Stow-on-the-Wold, Chipping Campden or Naunton. Turning south-west we usually pass over Broadway Tower and soon witness the most dramatic scenery the Cotswolds has to offer – the escarpment along its western edge where the ground falls sharply away to the valley of the Severn. Gentle hills become chiselled cliffs, the plateau drops away and the natural landscape suddenly meets the human landscape of towns and cities such as Cheltenham and Gloucester.

Climb higher, to 1500ft, and the Cotswolds starts to resemble a tapestry of stunning rivers, limestone hamlets and imposing stately homes, all surrounded by jaw-dropping countryside.

Before starting this book I asked people who knew the Cotswolds well for their suggestions of special places I should photograph. I was surprised that nearly all of them had a favourite – their own secret place – that was usually well away from the normal well-trodden tourist route. A fireman from Gloucester airport suggested I photograph the Church of St Giles in Uley, "the prettiest church in the area". A shop assistant in Broadway suggested a western view of the Iron-Age fort near Little Sodbury, "a place close to my heart, never mentioned in guide books, stunning". Talking to people such as these made me realise why the Cotswolds remain such a firm favourite with those who know the area or live there. It's a place that they identify with strongly and one that imprints itself on their imagination and memory.

In the 25 years that I've been visiting the Cotswolds I have accumulated countless favourite places and views, from the peaceful tranquillity of the hillside village of Snowshill to the 30 houses that make up John Wood's Royal Crescent in Bath. There is so much that makes this a unique and unspoiled area of Britain. I hope to keep visiting the Cotswolds for the next 25 years and discover many more places to enjoy and photograph along the way.

David Goddard

PART ONE

AROUND CHELTENHAM AND GLOUCESTER

Cheltenham and Gloucester lie on the western edge of the Cotswolds where the river Severn and its tributaries have carved deep and wide valleys into the surrounding hills. The river Chelt flows largely under the town of Cheltenham before its confluence with the Severn at Wainlode's Hill. The Severn estuary at Gloucester gives access to the sea and the town has a long history as a port for the west of England. Cheltenham and Gloucester are thriving modern cities but they are within easy reach of unspoiled towns like Winchcombe which is tucked away into the Cotswold edge and is sheltered on three sides by pleasantly wooded hills. The local architecture is dominated by honey-coloured Cotswold stone which may be found in everything from medieval churches to Regency terraces. The combination of interesting historical sites with areas of outstanding natural beauty makes the Cotswolds a magnet for tourism.

The former spa town of Cheltenham (above) and (left) looking north-east across the town towards the racecourse in the distance.

CHELTENHAM

Cheltenham began its life as a quiet market town, but the discovery of a mineral rich spring in what is now Cheltenham Ladies' College in 1716 enabled the town to re-invent itself as a spa. At its height, which was achieved with the five-week visit of King George III in 1788, Cheltenham Spa rivalled Bath in its splendour. Much of the architecture and layout of today's town dates from this period. In the 19th century the passing trade attracted by the health-giving waters was gradually replaced by permanent residents; often typified, perhaps unfairly, as retired colonial officials suffering from liver complaints.

5

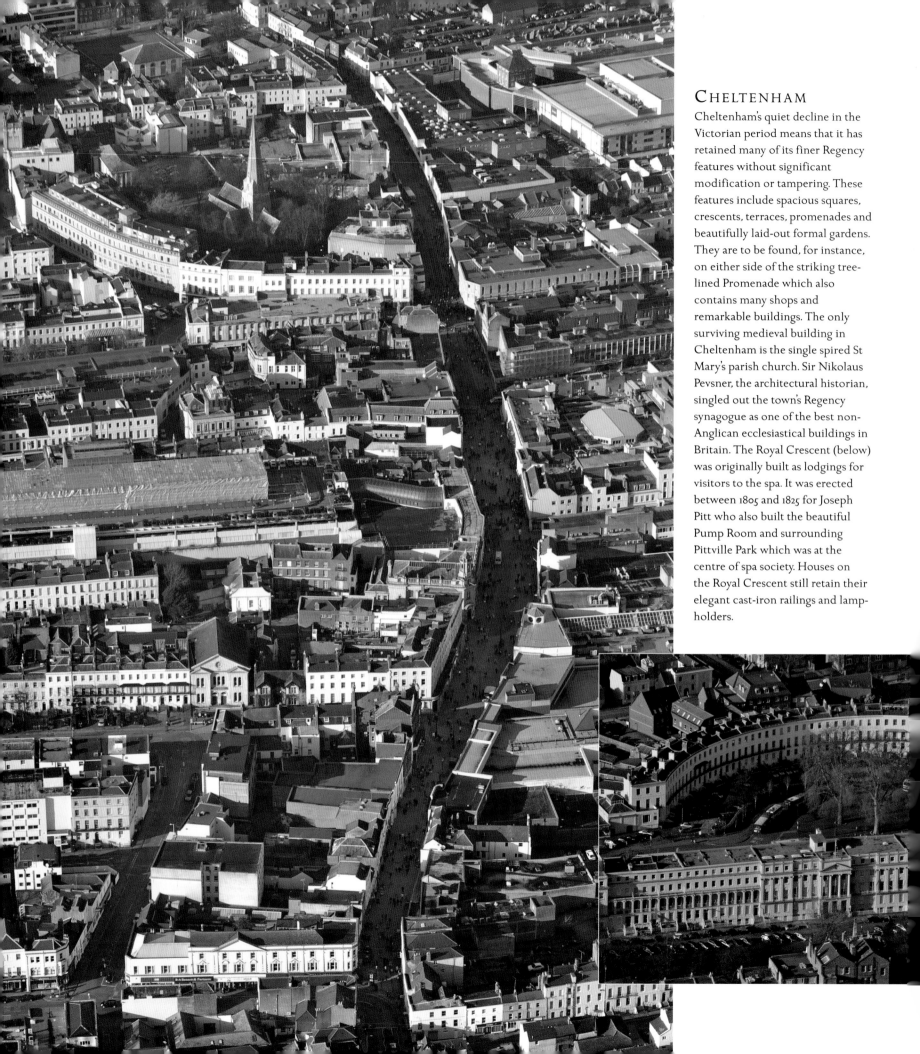

CHELTENHAM

Cheltenham's quiet decline in the Victorian period means that it has retained many of its finer Regency features without significant modification or tampering. These features include spacious squares, crescents, terraces, promenades and beautifully laid-out formal gardens. They are to be found, for instance, on either side of the striking tree-lined Promenade which also contains many shops and remarkable buildings. The only surviving medieval building in Cheltenham is the single spired St Mary's parish church. Sir Nikolaus Pevsner, the architectural historian, singled out the town's Regency synagogue as one of the best non-Anglican ecclesiastical buildings in Britain. The Royal Crescent (below) was originally built as lodgings for visitors to the spa. It was erected between 1805 and 1825 for Joseph Pitt who also built the beautiful Pump Room and surrounding Pittville Park which was at the centre of spa society. Houses on the Royal Crescent still retain their elegant cast-iron railings and lamp-holders.

The first recorded horse races at Cheltenham date from 1815 and nowadays the Cheltenham Festival (established in 1902) brings far more people to the town than any other form of tourism. The highlight of the festival is the Cheltenham Gold Cup which is at present the most valuable non-handicap horse race in Britain; in 2010 the total prize fund was £475,000. Winners of the Gold Cup have included Arkle, Golden Miller, Kauto Star and Mill House. The racecourse provides a home for the summer music festival and the south terminus of the Gloucestershire-Warwickshire heritage railway can be found there. Beyond the racecourse Cheltenham hosts several major festivals each year, including ones devoted to music, science and literature.

On a more modern note, the doughnut-shaped Government Communication Headquarters (GCHQ) building, home to the government surveillance programme, is also located in the western suburbs of the town.

Highnam Court

The original house at Highnam Court was seriously damaged in the Civil War and the present building, completed in 1658, is one of the few great houses dating from the Commonwealth period (1649-1660). The designer was probably Ernest Carter, a pupil of Inigo Jones. The Highnam Estate was acquired by the artist, musician and art collector Thomas Gambier Parry in 1838. Parry worked on the gardens from 1840 to 1874 but they fell into decline thereafter. Restoration work began in 1994 and the gardens have now been sensitively restored. The oval rose garden includes over 2,000 roses and there are 60,000 spring flowering bulbs.

COMPTON ABDALE

Compton Abdale is located in the Colne Valley and in the past sat on important trans-Cotswolds routes such as the "salt way" and the old London Road. Today it is just off the A40. The village's former role in transport is reflected in an old coaching inn called The Puesdown Inn and in the good-sized parish church of St Oswald's; this dates from the 13th century and features some unusual gargoyles. Also notable in the village is a stone water conduit carved in the shape of a crocodile's head; this has been delivering water to the village for at least 150 years and was recently restored.

HAILES

Outside the village of Hailes are the remains of a Cistercian abbey. During the 13th century the abbey came into possession of a relic of the Holy Blood of Christ which then drew vast numbers of pilgrims to the area. In 1539 the abbey was handed over to the king's agents as part of the Dissolution of the Monasteries and fell into disrepair when the lead was removed from its roof. All that now remains of the abbey are parts of the cloisters but the plan of the church is preserved by strategically-sited trees. Nearby is a 12th-century church which preserves some interesting medieval wall paintings.

WINCHCOMBE

The quiet and unassuming town of
Winchcombe was one of the seats
of the Saxon kings of Mercia and
was later a county town until it was
absorbed by Gloucestershire. In the
middle ages its abbey was a place of
pilgrimage for devotees of St
Kenelm the martyr. Most of the
buildings that distinguish the town
today are the legacy of the
Cotswolds wool trade. The town
has also benefited from its
proximity to Sudeley Castle. This
dates from the 10th century but
most of its surviving buildings are
Elizabethan. In the Tudor period,
the castle became the home of
Catherine Parr, the last wife of
Henry VIII; her marble tomb
designed by Sir Gilbert Scott is in
the chapel. Sudeley was Prince
Rupert's headquarters for a time in
the Civil War but suffered a decline
thereafter. Since the mid 19th
century the castle's owners have
been dedicated to restoring it and
its gardens to their former glory.

At the centre of Winchcombe is St Peter's, a justly celebrated example of a Cotswolds "wool" church. The original Norman church was rebuilt in the Perpendicular style between 1460 and 1470. The west tower has three stages and is surmounted by battlements, pinnacles and gargoyles. A series of grotesque heads adorn many parts of the exterior and a gilded weathercock was added in 1874.

GLOUCESTER

This prosperous city developed mostly on the eastern bank of the river Severn and dates back to Roman times. Some parts of the original Roman town wall have been traced as well as Roman coins and other remains. Sheltered by the Cotswolds to the east, by the Forest of Dean to the west and by the Malvern Hills to the north-west Gloucester sits at a natural confluence of trade routes.

Dominating the skyline even today, Gloucester's cathedral has its origins in an abbey founded in 681 and is the burial place of King Edward II. In the middle ages it was a centre for pilgrimage. Gloucester's prosperous history as a trading centre, inland port and spa can be glimpsed in the many fine buildings and churches that grace the city.

GLOUCESTER DOCKS

The docks were opened in 1827 and gave direct access by seagoing vessels to the Severn Estuary via a 16-mile ship canal. This meant that goods could be transferred to canal barges for transportation throughout the Midlands canal system. The docks and its warehouses were further expanded in 1848 to cope with increased corn imports following the repeal of the Corn Laws. By the 1980s most commercial traffic had died away and the docks have now been reveloped to provide spacious accommodation and ample leisure facilities. The survival of the old warehouses makes the Main Basin a popular location for period drama; fans of *The Onedin Line* will find Biddle's Warehouse familiar.

GREAT WITCOMBE

The Roman villa at Great Witcombe was probably built during the first century AD, and occupied until the fifth century. The main living quarters are in a large eastern wing and a long connecting gallery leads to a "leisure" wing containing a bath house and temple. The villa is built into the side of a hill which features several small streams and natural springs. It is thought that these water supplies formed the basis for fountains and other water features in the villa's gardens. The site was originally excavated in the 19th century and unfortunately has not been well preserved since then. The mosaic floor of the bath house, decorated with fish and sea creatures, can however still be seen inside a modern protective building.

WITHINGTON

Withington is a small village tucked into a fold of
the hills but its many interesting buildings speak
of a prosperous and varied history. A large Roman
villa once stood in the area and a mosaic
pavement from it is now housed in the British
Museum. In the middle ages the manor of
Withington was held by the bishops of Worcester
and several of its buildings date back to the 15th
century. The old schoolhouse was formerly a
courthouse. The Mill Inn looks as though it
should have a water wheel as it sits next to the
river Coln, but surprisingly the present inn dates
from the 1960s when it was built from weathered
stone recovered from Northleach Prison. At the
centre of the village is a well-preserved Norman
church. The exterior has many Norman features
including a solid tower and splendid south
doorway but unfortunately the interior was
rather over-enthusiastically cleaned up during
the Victorian period. To the right of the main
doorway there is a well preserved and ornate "tea
caddy" tomb. Inside, the memorial to the Howe
Family, with the names and dates of the parents
and their eight children, is particularly striking.
Near the church is the old manor house with a
medieval dovecote in its garden.

COLESBOURNE PARK

The rather scattered village of Colesbourne can be found in the wooded Churn valley. Colesbourne Park features numerous exotic trees as a result of the enthusiasm of a 19th century squire, Henry Elwes. A keen botanist and forester, he scoured the world for specimen trees and planted many of them on his land at Charlton Abbots. More traditional timber from the Colesbourne estate provided the bowsprit and masts of the restored SS *Great Britain*, Brunel's famous passenger steamship. The village church has a Perpendicular tower and in the interior there is a remarkable vase-shaped 15th-century stone pulpit.

NAUNTON

Naunton lies in the upper Windrush valley. Its church has an imposing Perpendicular tower complete with pinnacles and gargoyles. In the interior there is a carved 15th-century stone pulpit and a font from about the same period. The village has been a centre for sheep-rearing since it became monastic land in the middle ages. Naunton's other principle industry in former times was the production of stone roofing slates; at one time 30,000 tiles per week were dug from thin stone seams in nearby mines. Naunton's unusual dovecote, erected in 1660, incorporates four gables round a central turret.

GUITING POWER

Temple Guiting and Guiting Power are situated close together in the upper reaches of the Windrush valley. The word "guiting" denotes a spring or other powerful water source. Temple Guiting gets its name from the time in the 12th century when the manor was owned by the Knights Templar. Temple Guiting Manor was described by Pevsner as "One of the finest, if not the very best of the small Cotswold Tudor manor houses". Guiting Power is named after the Le Poer family who held lands in the area in the 13th and 14th centuries. The village centres on a triangular-shaped green confusingly known as The Square. In the centre of the green is a war memorial which echoes a medieval market cross in its design.

To the south-east of the village lies Guiting Grange, a stylish house first constructed in the middle of the 19th century, set amongst parkland. St Mary's church in Temple Guiting is built in an unusual combination of medieval and Georgian classical styles. The well-lit interior features a striking Georgian decalogue mounted over the south door which was created in 1748. The ornately painted set of wooden panels represent the Ten Commandments, the Creed and the Lord's Prayer. In the fields around Temple Guiting it should be possible to spot heritage flocks of Cotswold lion sheep. This large, white-faced, hornless breed was particularly prized in the middle ages for its long fleece, high growth rate and heavy wool clip.

AROUND CIRENCESTER

The open limestone countryside of the Cotswolds made the area attractive to Iron Age farmers as it was relatively easy to plough. In the middle ages improved horse plough technology made lowland areas more accessible and the Cotswolds became one of the country's prime sheep-rearing centres. English wool was a highly valued commodity and Cotswolds towns and villages grew rich on its trade. The industrial revolution led to a decline in the fortunes of the Cotswolds that was not halted until modern times. Today's farming is a mixture of arable and cattle rearing but it is no longer the major source of income for people who live in the Cotswolds.

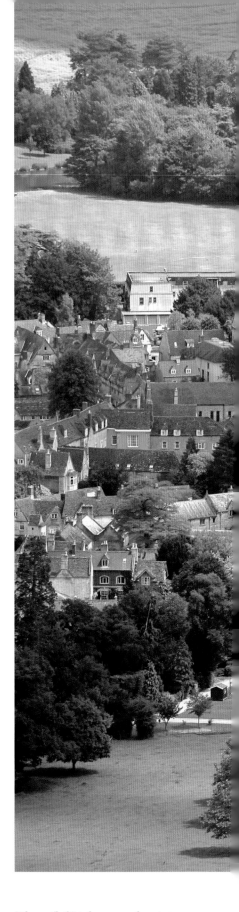

Bibury (left) is home to the picturesque Arlington Row weavers' cottages on the banks of the river Coln. Just a few miles away lies Cirencester (above) an important Roman settlement.

The quiet town of Bibury is typical of many in this area. Its heyday was during the 17th-century wool boom. Many of its buildings date from this period and many were rescued from decline in the 19th century. In contrast, Cirencester has been an important city since the Roman era when it stood at the junction of three major roads: the Fosse Way, the Ermin Way and Akeman Street. The

only visible remnants of the Roman city in modern Cirencester are part of the old wall and a large turf-covered amphitheatre. The town's prosperity in the middle ages was aided by the presence of a large abbey but it eventually grew to pre-eminence in the wool trade. Cirencester remains a busy market town that serves as an important centre for life in the southern Cotswolds.

CIRENCESTER

Two features dominate the town of Cirencester, the Church of St John the Baptist and Cirencester Park. The oldest part of the church dates from 1115 but it grew as the town and its associated religious communities prospered. The east window dates from around 1300 and its glass from the 15th century. The 1150 St Catherine's Chapel contains a wall painting of St Christopher carrying the Christ Child, and vaulting from 1508. The nave was completely rebuilt between 1515 and 1530 and is a fine example of late Perpendicular Gothic architecture. The 15th-century tower features exceptionally large buttresses. The south porch adjoining the market place is a standalone building known locally as the "Town Hall".

Occupying some 3,000 acres Cirencester Park is laid out geometrically according to Baroque ideas about landscaping. The scheme was begun by the first Earl of Bathurst in 1714-18 and is still part of the Bathurst estate. The poet Alexander Pope advised the Earl and his contribution is commemorated in a small rusticated shelter known as Pope's Seat. Other features added by the Earl include the hexagon, a Doric column surmounted by a statue of Queen Anne and the Gothic folly of Alfred's Hall. At the town end of the park can be found the award-winning Corinium Museum which explores Cirencester's Roman heritage. The park is home to the historic Cirencester Park Polo founded in 1894 and regarded as one of the finest polo grounds in the world.

BARNSLEY

There is an Iron Age settlement in Barnsley Park as well as a Roman villa dating from around AD360. A Saxon village, called *Bearmodeslea* (Bearmod's glade) was established by about 577. By the 11th century, according to the Domesday Book, the village's population stood at 24. The village became royal property under Henry VIII after the Dissolution of the Monasteries, but it was eventually acquired by the Bouchier family in 1548. The Bouchiers were the principle landowners for the next two hundred years and were responsible for building Barnsley House, Church Cottage and parts of the Church farm. Barnsley's population peaked in 1821 at 318; during the First World War the village had an estimated 200 inhabitants, of whom six lost their lives in the conflict.

Barnsley village is chiefly noted for Barnsley House Garden, above and left. Barnsley House itself dates from 1697 when it was built for a local landowner. It later became a parsonage but came to fame when famous garden designer and writer Rosemary Verey moved into the house and took on the development of its gardens in the 1950s. She created a variety of garden types including an 18th-century herb garden, a knot garden, a laburnum walk, a temple with a pool and a vegetable garden. The gardens have received worldwide attention and inspired the Prince of Wales' gardens at nearby Highgrove House. The beautifully maintained garden is open to the public throughout the year.

BIBURY

Bibury dates back to Saxon times but the bulk of the village owes its existence to the 17th-century wool trade. The river Coln flows through the village providing both trout fishing and, in the past, power for various mills. The picturesque Arlington Row is a terrace of weavers' cottages that once housed workers from nearby Arlington Mill; it probably began life as a monastic barn. Rack Isle, in front of the cottages and now a bird sanctuary, used to have racks on it for drying wool. William Morris declared Bibury to be the loveliest village in England and its combination of Cotswold vernacular architecture and tranquil waterways have made it a magnet for visitors ever since.

The parish church of Saint Mary is Saxon in origin and in spite of later additions many of its original features still survive. These include a gravestone embedded in the north wall. The interior of the church features a stained-glass window designed by Karl Parsons in 1927 depicting a coach. Alongside the traditional wool bale graves in Bibury churchyard can be found the Bisley Piece, a relic of the time in the 14th century when the people of Bisley angered a Pope. Forbidden to bury their dead in their own churchyard they had to travel 15 miles to use the one at Bibury.

COLN ST ALDWYNS

The river Coln adds both its name and its charm to the picturesque village of Coln St Aldwyns. The village green is sheltered by a large horse chestnut tree and there is a welcoming local inn. The churchyard is well-maintained and inside the church can be found memorial windows commemorating the 19th-century church reformer John Keble and his father. John Keble Senior was the vicar from 1782-1835 and his son served as his curate.

CHEDWORTH

Chedworth combines sites of both ancient and modern interest. Opposite the Seven Tuns Inn a spring emerges from a wall whilst elsewhere in the village there is a sculpture of the Virgin and Child carved by Helen Rock in 1911. Not far from the village is Chedworth Roman villa. Discovered in 1864 and dating from AD120-400, the beautifully preserved remains include mosaic pavements (one depicting the four seasons), bath suites and a hypocaust.

NORTHLEACH

Northleach was one of the most important
Cotswold wool towns in the middle ages and its
heyday as a medieval trading centre can still be
glimpsed in its market square and many half-
timbered buildings. The most obvious legacy of
Northleach's pre-eminence in the wool trade is its
church. This was largely rebuilt in the Perpendicular
style in the 15th century and is a magnificent
example of the style and period. The pinnacled
south porch is said to be without equal in England
and its tower combines both elegance and strength.
The generous windows in the clerestory provide
ample light for such features as a 15th-century
goblet-shaped pulpit and a new ceiling designed
by Sir Basil Spence. Northleach did not have a
generous enough water supply to take advantage
of the Industrial Revolution and it went into
serious decline during the early 19th century.
In 1831 there were only 126 occupied houses and
795 inhabitants. It is hard to imagine such a dismal
prospect today thanks to the beautiful and
generous architecture of the town largely built
during the boom years of the wool trade.

HAMPNETT

Hampnett centres on a large village green and is
close to the source of the river Leach. Its parish
church of St George is largely Norman but
during the 1880s its interior was decorated with
extensive stencilwork. It could be argued such
designs obscure the clean lines of the Norman
church but on the other hand, during the
Norman and Medieval periods, most churches
would have had similarly decorated walls.

FARMINGTON

The village of Farmington stands on high
ground between the valleys of the river Leach
and the Sherborne Brook. The principal house
in the village is Farmington Lodge. This is
a mixture of 18th and 19th-century styles and
is fronted by four sizeable Doric columns.
A rather more graceful aspect of the village
green is an octagonal pumphouse topped by an
elegant cupola. The church is Norman in origin
and still retains many Norman features such
as its south doorway and chancel arch. The
Perpendicular tower was added in the 15th
century but is well integrated with the earlier
buildings.

RENDCOMB

Rendcomb is an estate village
which used to serve Rendcomb
Court. Rendcomb Court is an
Italianate mansion built during
the 19th century by Thomas Cubitt.
Since 1920 it has been a boarding
school catering for pupils from the
ages of 3 to 18. The parish church of
St Peter dates largely from the 14th
century and its chief glory is a
carved 12th-century font. The font
was created between 1130 and 1140
and shows images of the twelve
apostles; eleven are identifiable
by symbols but the twelfth,
representing Judas, is blank with
only a pair of feet showing.

CALMSDEN

The hamlet of Calmsden is distinguished by a rare 14th-century wayside cross. Mounted on sturdy stepped stones the upright is still visible but the cross piece has disappeared (bottom left in the photograph). A spring emerges above ground nearby and a row of estate cottages built during the 19th century also add charm to the area. The Old House dates from the 16th century and is now run as a hotel.

PINBURY PARK

Pinbury Park consists of a large 16th-century house enclosed by a wooded landscape. In the 1930s the park was home to the poet John Masefield, while in the late 19th century it captivated Ernest Gimson and the Barnsley brothers, associates of William Morris. When the three men moved to Pinbury in 1894, the house was dilapidated but they used their Arts & Crafts principles and skills to restore and extend the house and its gardens.

NORTH CERNEY

North Cerney consists of a single
street with views across the Churn
valley. The church with its
saddleback tower was largely
rebuilt in the 1470s following a
fire but it retains some Norman
features. The interior is said to
be one of the best furnished in
England and has a finely carved
stone pulpit. The churchyard
features 14th-century and 16th-
century graffiti on the exterior
wall; one carving seems to be of
a mythical beast with a lion's head
and tail but the body of a man
known as a manticore. The primary
school was founded in 1844 and
there is also a Methodist Chapel
dating from 1891.

PART THREE
NORTH COTSWOLDS

The area around Stow-on-the-Wold is rich in beautiful villages and picturesque landscapes, from the rolling wolds themselves to the many attractive, sheltered valleys provided by the rivers Windrush, Eye and Dikler. The area has been settled since prehistoric times, as is evidenced by the numerous tumuli, hill forts and barrows but the buildings and settlements that stand out in the visitor's mind are the ones that grew out of the wool trade that prospered here from the late middle ages onwards. Constructed from the local honey-coloured stone these dwellings represent a vision of the countryside that has become quintessentially English. Great houses and architectural follies sit beside, and harmonise with, humble workers' cottages and devoutly built churches. The landscape is lightly and variously wooded and the fields have been shaped by the needs of centuries of wool production.

St Edward's Hall (left) in Stow-on-the-Wold was built in 1878 and stands in the town's large market square. Chipping Campden (above) is noted for its elegant high street.

WOOL'S RICHES

The wealth of the Cotswolds is founded on wool. Wool production in the area dates from at least the Roman period but until the middle ages most wool was exported as raw material for spinning and weaving in places like Ghent and Bruges. When Cotswold communities began spinning and weaving their own cloth new wealth poured into the area. The money paid for the great houses, the massive churches and even the labourers' cottages that give the Cotswolds their unique character. The area remained rich until the Industrial Revolution introduced "king cotton" as the material of choice for most clothing.

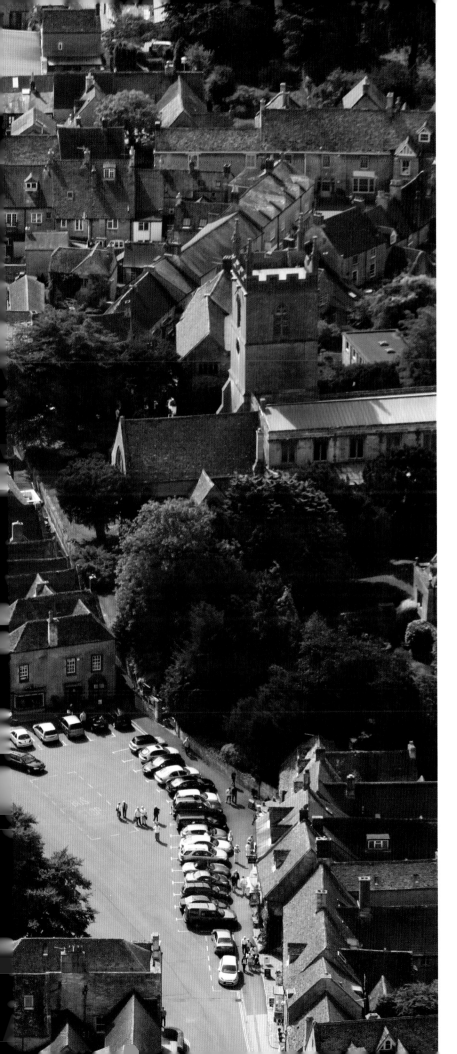

STOW-ON-THE-WOLD

Stow-on-the-Wold is, at 800ft, the highest town in the Cotswolds. A popular rhyme begins "Stow-on-the-Wold, where the wind blows cold" and the unusual shape of its market square is in part dictated by the need for stallholders to be protected from the wind. Despite its unpromising position Stow-on-the-Wold has been a thriving market town since at least 1107. At the centre of the town is the parish church of St Edward which was built between the 11th and the 15th centuries. It was restored in the 1680s after it had been used as a Civil War prison and extensively "improved" in 1847. Its tower, completed in 1447, is 88ft high and houses the heaviest peal of bells in Gloucestershire.

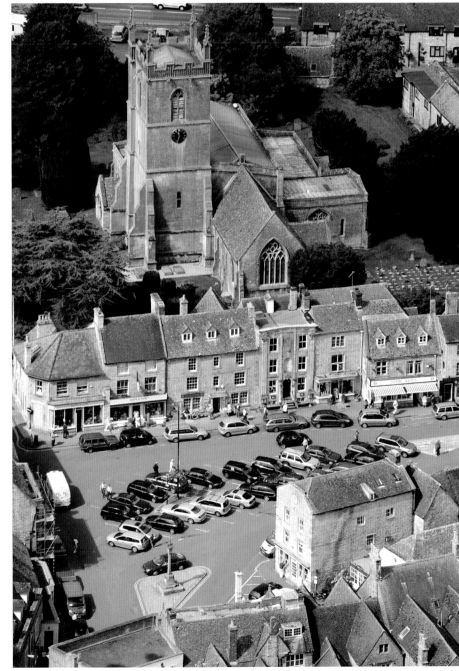

CHASTLETON

Chastleton House was built between 1607 and 1612 by the wealthy wool merchant Walter Jones. It remained in the possession of the same family for the next 400 years but they struggled to maintain the house. By the time the property was donated to the National Trust in 1991 the family's "make do and mend" approach meant that the interior of the house represented a virtual time capsule which preserved many aspects of life that would have been discarded or "improved" under other circumstances. In particular the house preserves textiles such as a striped wall or "dornix" hanging at the top of the east staircase together with early 17th-century "flamestitch" wall hangings that are almost unique.

BROADWELL

Broadwell had 46 inhabitants when it was mentioned in the Domesday Book in 1086. Parts of St Paul's church date from the early Norman period but in the later middle ages the estate belonged to the Benedictine order of monks. The large green was donated to the village by Lord Ashton in the late 20th century. A tributary of the Evenlode runs beside the green and the road crosses the stream via a shallow ford. The Manor House is a grade II listed building and dates largely from the 17th century with some 19th- and 20th-century additions.

LOWER SLAUGHTER

At one end of Lower Slaughter is a large mill pond which feeds a working waterwheel. The 19th-century mill is now a museum and houses one of only three unused millstones left in the country. St Mary's church was rebuilt in 1867 and has an imposing spire. Lower Slaughter Manor House dates from 1650 when it was built for Valentine Strong, the owner of a quarry at Little Barrington. The house has been remodelled since its construction but its grounds preserve one of the largest dovecotes in Gloucestershire. Several simply built footbridges span the river Eye in Lower Slaughter and a number of long-distance footpaths, including the Gloucestershire Way and the Heart of England Way, pass through the village.

UPPER SLAUGHTER

The village is grouped around
a small square with the church
alongside. The cottages that
comprise the Square were
reconstructed by Sir Edwin Lutyens
in 1906. The most imposing
building today is the gabled Manor
House, parts of which date from
the 15th century; the front is an
Elizabethan addition. St Peter's
church has Norman origins and a
15th-century tower. Some Norman
stonework has survived rather too
rigorous Victorian restorations.
Completely belying its bloodthirsty
sounding name, Upper Slaughter is
a double "thankful" village. All of
the men it sent to fight in the First
and Second World Wars returned
home alive.

LONGBOROUGH

Longborough is pleasantly situated on a hillside overlooking the Evenlode valley. Evidence of human settlement in Longborough goes back 5,000 years in the form of the long barrow that gives the village its name. A Roman settlement has also been found in the area. During the middle ages, local landowners wanted to knock down the settlement and disperse the villagers in favour of sheep but happily the village survived. The church of St James which stands at the heart of the village has a 13th-century tower with an added 15th-century upper section in the Perpendicular style, while the windows on the south porch are in the Decorated style characteristic of the 14th century. Since 1991 Longborough Festival Opera has staged productions at Banks' Fee Manor House. Starting out as an opera and picnic evening the productions now have their own theatre and range from Mozart to Wagner.

SEZINCOTE HOUSE

Sezincote House was designed by Samuel Pepys Cockerell in 1805 and along with
Brighton Pavilion it is a striking example of Neo-Mughal architecture – a 19th-
century reinterpretation of 16th and 17th-century Indian models. The dominant
colour at Sezincote is red sandstone, as its Indian inspirations would have been,
but the central minaret is copper-covered rather than white marble. The extra-large
windows have a typically Mughal arch-shape at the top. The interiors do not reflect
the exterior design and are more typically European in style. The landscape was
designed by Humphry Repton and combines a Renaissance-style garden with
elements of Hindu design such as a crescent bridge with columns.

MORETON-IN-MARSH

Moreton-in-Marsh straddles the Fosse Way; its position on various key transportation routes probably accounts for its existence and prosperity. During the 17th and 18th centuries Moreton-in-Marsh was on the main coaching route between London, Oxford, Worcester and Hereford. When coaching declined the town quickly moved on to railways.

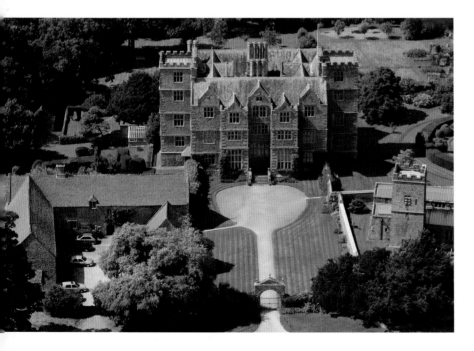

As a centre for travellers Moreton-in-Marsh is well provided with inns, one of which was used by Charles I during the Civil War. The Curfew Hall on the corner of Oxford Street still has its original 1633 curfew bell hanging in its tower; the bell was in daily use until 1860. Moreton-in-Marsh received its first charter for a weekly market in 1227 and the town has had a fair since 1267. The administrative centre for collecting market tolls and fees was the Market Hall. The splendid neo-Tudor style Redesdale Market Hall in Moreton-in-Marsh was built at the comparatively late date of 1887.

Moreton's wide main street, once part of the Roman Fosse Way, shows the town's importance as a route centre and as a market town. Every Tuesday the town hosts one of the largest open-air markets in the Cotswolds.

BOURTON-ON-THE-HILL

The village of Bourton-on-the-Hill was once owned by the abbots of Westminster who also had large sheep runs on the nearby downs. The wealth created by the 15th-century wool industry enabled the building of a particularly fine clerestory on the church. The three stage tower also dates from the Perpendicular period but the weighty arched columns of the interior reveal its Norman origins. The church also preserves a bell-metal bushel and peck from 1816. These standard measures were once required by law in every church so that they could be used for the gathering of tithes and for settling disputes. At the top of the hill is a substantial 18th-century coaching inn; the village also contains many fine 17th and 18th-century cottages.

BLOCKLEY

Blockley was one of the first villages in England to produce its own electricity, thanks to the power of the Blockley Brook. In previous centuries the brook provided the energy for corn mills, silk throwers and even wood saws. Six mills once operated in the village although only one is still open; the beautiful Mill Dene garden has been created around another one. Parts of the church date from the Norman period but the tower was only added in 1725. At the height of the silk boom in the late 19th century around 600 people were employed making silk for ribbons. Many of the terraced cottages on the northern edge of the village were once occupied by silk weavers.

BATSFORD

Algernon Bertram Freeman-Mitford (later 1st Lord Redesdale) travelled widely in the Far East before inheriting the Batsford Estate in the latter part of the 19th century. He had become fascinated by bamboos and other exotic plants and, after rebuilding Batsford Park House, he turned his attention to planting exotic trees in its gardens. He also explored ideas about wild gardens and extensively altered the landscape he inherited. In the 20th century the 2nd Lord Dulverton continued to expand the estate's role as an arboretum and Batsford became a charitable trust in 1984. The Batsford Arboretum now houses one of the largest private collections of trees and shrubs in the country and is open to the public throughout the year, except during the winter months.

CHIPPING CAMPDEN

The word "chipping" relates to an Old English word meaning cattle and it was as a wool and cattle market that the village first grew up. The many fine houses in the village are evidence of its successful trading past. Grevel House was built for William Grevel in about 1380 and features striking Perpendicular-style two-storey windows. The Market Hall was built in 1627 and was intended for the sale of cheese, butter and poultry in a period when the wool trade was in decline. The row of

almshouses just below St James' church date from 1612; they originally cost £1,000 and are still used today to house 12 Campden pensioners. Next to the church are the lodges and gateway to Campden House. These are the only remains of the original buildings as the rest were burned down during the Civil War. St James' church is a significant local landmark. It is built in the Perpendicular style and features a 15th-century pinnacled tower and some marble monuments.

BROAD CAMPDEN

Broad Campden is less than a mile south of Chipping Campden and is hidden away in the lightly wooded valley of a small stream that feeds into the Knee Brook a little further east. The earliest mention of the village is in 1216; a good number of the older houses and cottages still have thatched roofs. A Norman chapel, which was converted into a house by Charles Ashbee in 1905, dates from the 12th century. The church of St Michael's and All Angels is Victorian in origin and features an altar rail designed by Ashbee. The Quaker meeting house was built in 1663 making it one of the oldest meeting houses in the country; it still preserves many of its original furnishings. Bledington lies on the Oxfordshire Way footpath and you can walk westwards up on the wolds via Wyck Beacon and down to Bourton-on-the-Water, or south-eastwards down the valley to Bruern Abbey and on to Shipston-under-Wychwood.

NORTHWICK PARK

At the centre of Northwick Park is a grade I listed building which dates back to 1686. This was converted into luxury apartments in the late 1980s along with various stables and outbuildings. Since that time modern buildings have been added in a compatible style to make up a luxurious gated community. During the Second World War the Northwick Park estate housed the American Emergency Hospital which covered 72 acres and catered for wounded soldiers, sailors and airmen. American medical services arrived at Northwick Park in 1942 and left in 1946.

WILLERSEY

With its village green, duckpond and ancient church, Willersey is a typical lowland English village. It is on the edge of the Cotwolds but its mellow-stoned, well-proportioned houses link it firmly with the uplands. In the middle ages the Abbots of Evesham had a summer residence in Willersey and later William Roper, the son-in-law of Sir Thomas More, held the manor. King Charles II gave the Penderel family a house here in thanks for their help in his escape after the Battle of Worcester. Most of the houses in the village date from this period or later, although the church dates largely from the 14th century.

SAINTBURY

This small village is ranged along the side of Saintbury Hill. The name Saintbury probably refers to a Saxon holy man called Cada who built a small cell nearby. The Norman church of St Nicholas still preserves some fragments of a former Saxon building and commands a fine view of the Vale of Evesham. The interior features a barrel-vaulted roof from the Queen Anne period plus Jacobean altar rails and pulpit. The village itself has a fine cross which stands at the crossroads to the north. The lower part dates from the 15th century whilst the Maltese cross and sundial were added in 1848.

BROADWAY

Broadway, as its name suggests, has a wide main street and the village was once an important staging post on the London to Worcester route. A new turnpike road was opened in 1736 and at one time seven coaches passed through the village each day. Many of the fine buildings along Broadway's main street began their lives as inns to serve the passing trade. With the coming of the railways the coach trade died away but Broadway had its own station and it quickly became a stopping off point for exploration of the Cotswolds. JM Barrie, Vaughan Williams, Edward Elgar and the American artists Edwin Austin Abbey and John Singer Sargent all made use of Broadway as did Arts & Crafts movement luminaries such as William Morris and Gordon Russell; Russell established a furniture workshop in the village which is now a museum. The picturesque village is regarded by many as the finest large village in the Cotswolds.

The church of Saint Eadburgha in Broadway is situated in a quiet lane at the foot of Snowshill, to the south of the village. This has been a site of worship since Saxon times. The relatively remote location of the church may have been as a result of the plague – an attempt to keep the churchyard as far away as possible from nearby settlements. The present building dates from the 12th century and has some very fine medieval and Jacobean woodwork.

BUCKLAND

The secluded village of Buckland lies just below the Cotswolds escarpment at the foot of Burhill. The rectory is thought to be the oldest in England and has a stately timbered hall that dates from the 15th century. The Church of St Michael features an east window which contains 15th-century glass reputed to have come from Hailes Abbey when it was dissolved. John Wesley preached in the church and William Morris attended services there when he was visiting Buckland. Morris liked the glass in the east window so much that he personally paid for its re-leading.

BROADWAY TOWER

Broadway Tower stands on top of a beacon hill that on a clear day can provide views of 13 counties. The idea for the tower came from Capability Brown but it was designed and built by James Wyatt in 1798. The "Saxon Tower" features an eclectic mixture of architectural components ranging from turrets and battlements to gargoyles and balconies. Since its completion it has attracted many artists and the building now houses a museum.

STANTON

Stanton is essentially a single street village and is claimed by many to be one of the oldest in the Cotswolds. Most of the houses date from the 17th century but the village was extensively restored by the architect Sir Philip Stott after he purchased large tracts of it just before the First World War. Stott modernised many features but set up covenants to prevent the worst excesses of the 20th century from taking hold in the village, and as a result Stanton often provides a backdrop for period film and television shoots. Parts of Stanton's church date back to the 12th century and it features both a 14th century and a Jacobean pulpit. It has an elegant spire and some of its windows date from the 15th century.

SNOWSHILL

There have been settlements near Snowshill since the Bronze Ages. A barrow nearby contained a famous collection of weapons now in the British Museum. The main part of the current Snowshill Manor house dates from around 1500 but there were alterations and extensions in the 17th and 18th centuries. In 1919 the almost derelict building was bought and restored by Charles Paget Wade, who needed somewhere to present his collection of 22,000 examples of craftsmanship. Amassed between 1900 and 1951 the diverse collection illustrates Wade's idea that objects embody the spirit of the craftsman who made them. The collection includes automatons, butter stamps, bicycles, children's toys, clocks, cow bells, locks and 26 suits of Samurai armour.

STANWAY

The village of Stanway is dominated by the gatehouse to Stanway House where a mixture of Gothic, Renaissance and Dutch styles are given a pleasing unity by the local stone. Stanway House was built during the 1580s on the site of an earlier manor house. It is mostly Jacobean in style and has a remarkable 60 pane oriel window. The grounds contain a restored water garden which features the highest fountain in England; an impressive tithe barn dating from 1370; and a log-fired brewing house. The church of St Peter retains its Jacobean pulpit but elsewhere has suffered badly at the hands of Victorian restorers. Opposite the driveway to Stanway house is a thatched cricket pavilion mounted on saddle stones. This unusual building was a gift to the village from JM Barrie, the author of *Peter Pan*.

65

PART FOUR

SOUTH COTSWOLDS

The South Cotswolds area is accessible via the M4 and M5 corridors, and contains many architectural and scenic gems. Historic market towns offer numerous distractions from craft and antique shops via elegant tea rooms to events and festivals such as the traditional Mop Fairs in Chipping Sodbury or the food and drink festival in Tetbury. The world's largest military air show, the Royal International Air Tattoo, takes place at RAF Fairford in mid-July every year. There are opportunities for walking holidays along the Cotswold Way national trail, art history can be pursued through William Morris's home at Lechlade and the area is teeming with great houses, fascinating gardens, wetland areas and patches of ancient woodland. The honey-coloured stone of the northern area becomes creamier in the south of the area.

Dodington House (left) is an elegant 18th-century mansion situated in parkland designed by Capability Brown. The beautiful city of Bath (above) is famous for its splendid Georgian architecture.

FINE HOUSES AND GRANDEUR

With one or two exceptions the Cotswolds have been prosperous for more than 600 years. The first boom in the middle ages involved wool but towns in and around the Cotswolds have prospered greatly as a result of quarrying, transport or health tourism. This means that the visitor can find a great deal of fine architecture in many different styles and from many different periods in one relatively small area. This includes both the vernacular architecture of the towns and villages as well as the more ornate grand houses and stately homes which dot the beautiful Cotswold landscape.

BATH

Bath is a city that has had two major heydays: the first was during the Roman occupation when the town of *Aqua Sulis* grew up around the natural hot springs in the area, and the second during the Regency and Georgian periods when the craze for "taking the waters" made Bath the centre of fashion and one of the largest cities in England. Substantial reminders of both periods can still be seen in the city today.

Bath is on the very edge of the Cotswold hills and the stone in this area is usually described as creamy rather than golden. The Roman temple and baths, the cathedral and the city's famous terraces are all built from locally quarried limestone. Apart from the Roman baths and the temple the ancient city of Bath largely disappeared during the Saxon period; throughout the middle ages the city was largely in royal and monastic hands. The spa trade began to revive after the Dissolution of the Monasteries but it was not until the period after the Civil War (1642-51) that Bath began to be a health centre for the aristocracy.

BATH

As the fashion for taking the waters at Bath gathered pace during the Georgian and Regency periods new quarters of the city were opened up. The architects John Wood the Elder (1704-1754) and his son John Wood the Younger (1728-1782) laid out the new quarters in the neo-Classical style in streets and squares, using identical façades to create vistas on a palatial scale. Justly famous examples of the style can be seen in Lansdowne Terrace, the Royal Cresent and the Circus. Much of the creamy gold Bath stone, which was used for construction throughout the city, came from limestone mines at Combe Down and Bathampton Down. By 1801 the population of the city had reached 40,000, making it one of the largest centres of population in Britain. Bath continues to attract visitors who wish to enjoy its natural thermal waters, as seen below at the open-air rooftop pool at Thermae Bath Spa.

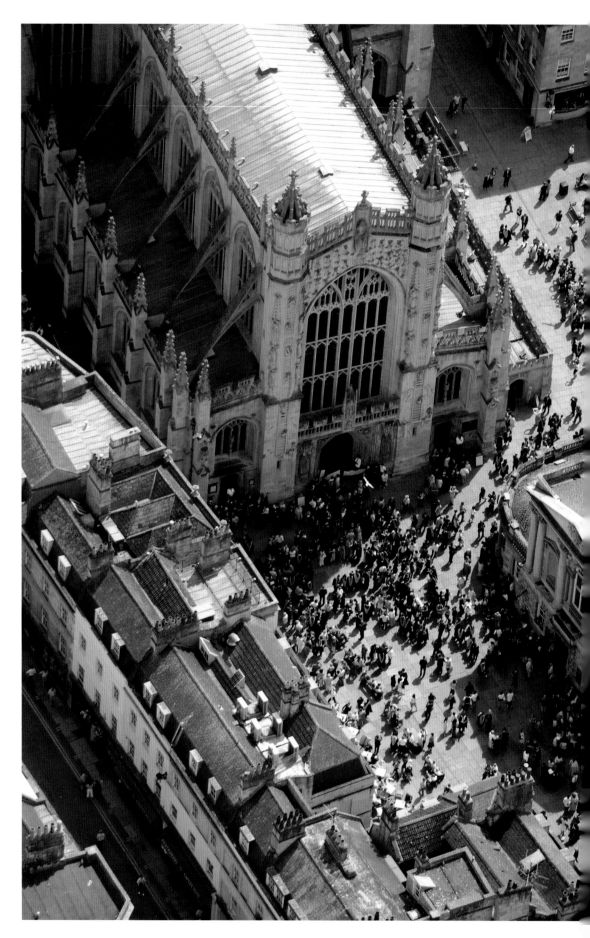

In the middle of Bath can be found the old Roman baths and the abbey church. By the 15th century, Bath's original abbey church was badly dilapidated and in need of repairs. In 1500 it was decided to rebuild the church on a smaller scale; a project that was completed just in time for the Dissolution of Bath Priory in 1539. The abbey church then fell into disrepair but it was restored as the city's parish church during the Elizabethan period and completed in 1611. It is one of the largest examples of Perpendicular Gothic architecture in the west country. Major restoration work included installation of fan vaulting in the nave. This was not merely a Victorian whim but a completion of the original design that had been abandoned due to cost.

MIDFORD CASTLE

Midford Castle is a folly built in 1775 for Henry Disney Roebuck from designs by John Carter. The house has a trefoil plan formed by three semi-circular towers and is in the Gothic style. The later addition of a porch makes the building look like a playing card club, a fact that has led to much fanciful speculation about the original funding of the house. Extensive renovation work was carried out in the 1960s, including extensive remodelling of the gardens, and the castle was briefly owned by the actor Nicolas Cage from 2007 to 2009.

GRITTLETON

The small village of Grittleton is dominated by the grade II listed building of Grittleton House School. This is a small independent school and children's daycare centre that caters for around 300 pupils and toddlers aged 2-16. The main building is a country house designed and built by James Thomson between 1832 and 1856. It is set in 30 acres of grounds. The building was converted into a school in 1967. The singer Jamie Cullum is a former pupil, as is the actress Angelica Mandy and the show jumper Tom Restorick.

BADMINTON

Badminton House is the home of the Beaufort family and is a particularly fine example of the Palladian style dating from the early 18th century. Its principal architect was William Kent who extended and renovated an existing building when the Beauforts relocated to Badminton after Raglan Castle was devastated in the Civil War. The rules of the game of Badminton – which had developed amongst army officers in India – were formalised at the house in 1873 and the standard sizes of its court are dictated by the size of the hall. The park is partly the work of Capability Brown and contains a Great Avenue that is several miles long. Badminton Deer Park is listed on the Register of Parks and Gardens of Special Historic Interest in England. The estate is also associated with the annual Badminton horse trials and, until fox-hunting was banned, with the Beaufort Hunt.

LYEGROVE HOUSE

This beautiful house and garden is approximately two miles east of Chipping Sodbury. It dates from the 17th century but was greatly altered in the the early 19th century. In 1927 the house was restored by GH Kitchin and Flemish-style gables and a Roman Doric porch were added for the Earl of Westmorland. Adjoining the house to the east is a courtyard with accommodation for servants. The stable block, seen below to the right of the main house, is surmounted by a cupola and has a date-stone of 1856. The interior of the house contains a fine Renaissance fireplace, dated 1633, and said to have been brought from Little Sodbury Manor; in the staircase hall, there is a 17th-century staircase assembled by GH Kitchin. The extensive gardens include three 20th-century walled formal gardens plus a 19th-century raised terrace walk, seen right, with crenellated walls and corner bastions.

DODINGTON PARK

Dodington Park, south-east of Chipping Sodbury, was acquired by the Codrington family in the late 16th century. The original house was Elizabethan and had a church attached. The family prospered in the 18th century as a result of investments in West Indian sugar and commissioned James Wyatt to rebuild the house between 1798 and 1813. The extensive grounds were laid out by Capability Brown around 1764 and later modified by William Emes and John Webb. The church was also rebuilt by Wyatt and a formal garden was added in 1930. The Codrington family moved out in 1980. The river Frome rises in the estate grounds and flows in a south-westerly direction through Bristol before joining the river Avon at Bristol harbour.

LITTLE SODBURY

This village lies between Chipping Sodbury to the west, Old Sodbury to the south and Badminton to the east. Little Sodbury Manor dates from 1420. Sir John Walsh inherited the property in 1504 and Henry VIII and Anne Boleyn stayed there in 1535 during their royal summer progress. The house was extended later in the century and again in the 16th century; it was restored in the 18th and 20th centuries. The gardens are extensive and feature terraces on several levels, a sunken garden, a formal garden, a kitchen garden and a Tudor bowling green. There is an overgrown water garden consisting of a series of ponds and waterfalls which was designed by Sir Harold Brakespear. Above Little Sodbury, on the Cotswold Way, is an Iron Age fort, left, that was also used and rebuilt by the Romans.

OLD SODBURY

Old Sodbury is built around a triangular village green and possesses a good selection of amenities. The Church of Saint John the Baptist stands slightly aloof from the green and is late Norman in origin. It contains two effigies of knights: the oldest is dated 1240 and is carved out of stone; the second, carved in wood, dates from the late 14th century. The churchyard features a number of old bale-tombs commemorating rich wool merchants.

HORTON

Horton is a linear village built up the bank of a steep hill on the Cotswold Edge. Horton Court is a stone-built manor house which preserves the remains of a 12th-century rectory with early Renaissance decorations. All that now remains of the rectory is its hall and a striking detached ambulatory. The ambulatory or loggia was built in 1527 for William Knight after his return from Italy. The Church of St James is 12th-century in origin and Perpendicular in style having been rebuilt in the 14th century and altered in the 15th and 16th centuries. It retains a Norman fort and a Jacobean pulpit and the churchyard has many local and Classical chest tombs which date from the 18th century.

HAWKESBURY

Hawkesbury is dominated by its 12th-century parish church. It is mainly in the Perpendicular style and built out of gold-coloured limestone. The Old Vicarage is an unusual L-shape and dates from the late 15th century. It features a two-storey gabled porch and a late 18th-century garden building with Gothic arched windows. Outside the village on the Cotswold Edge is the 100ft high Somerset Monument, right. This was erected in 1846 to commemorate General Lord Edward Somerset who served with distinction at Waterloo and died in 1842. Somerset was the nephew of the Sixth Duke of Beaufort whose family home is nearby.

WESTONBIRT

Westonbirt House was the property of the Holford family from 1665 until 1926. The present building is the third on the site and was constructed in 1863 and 1870 based on a design by Lewis Vulliamy. The exterior is in an Elizabethan style and features a symmetrical main block and asymmetric wings. The interiors are in a Classical style. Large formal terrace gardens surround the house and beyond them are 25 acres of ornamental woodlands. Since 1928, the house has been occupied by a girls' boarding school. Nearby is the Westonbirt Arboretum which was also created by members of the Holford family.

TETBURY AND HIGHGROVE

Tetbury is a large market town that features a magnificent 17th-century Market House; the Chipping Steps, where a livestock market used to take place; Gumstool Hill, the scene of annual Woolsack Races; a Court House which is now a Police Museum; and around 30 antiques shops. Overlooking the town is St Mary's church which was rebuilt in the Gothic style in the late 18th century; its spire is 186ft high (57m). The interior is illuminated by Perpendicular windows and features box pews, panelled galleries and two chandeliers. Highgrove House became the home of the Prince of Wales in 1980. It was chosen for its proximity to London and easy access to Wales and the west of England. The main house dates from the late 18th century and is in a neo-Classical style. It has four reception rooms, nine main bedrooms, a nursery wing and staff quarters. The Prince of Wales has devoted much of his time to the gardens and has created a wild garden, a formal garden and a walled kitchen garden. He has also planted many trees in the grounds.

WOTTON-UNDER-EDGE

The oldest building in Wotton-under-Edge is the timber-framed Ram Inn which is believed to date from 1350. The parish Church of St Mary the Virgin was consecrated in 1283 and possesses a fine late 14th-century tower. Inside the church is the Berkeley Tomb, an early 15th-century table tomb which bears life-sized brasses of Thomas, 10th Baron de Berkeley (1352-1417), and his wife, Margaret. The brasses are reputedly the best of their kind in England. One of the first grammar schools in the country was founded at Wotton by Katharine Lady Berkeley in 1384. The Church Street Almshouses were built in 1638.

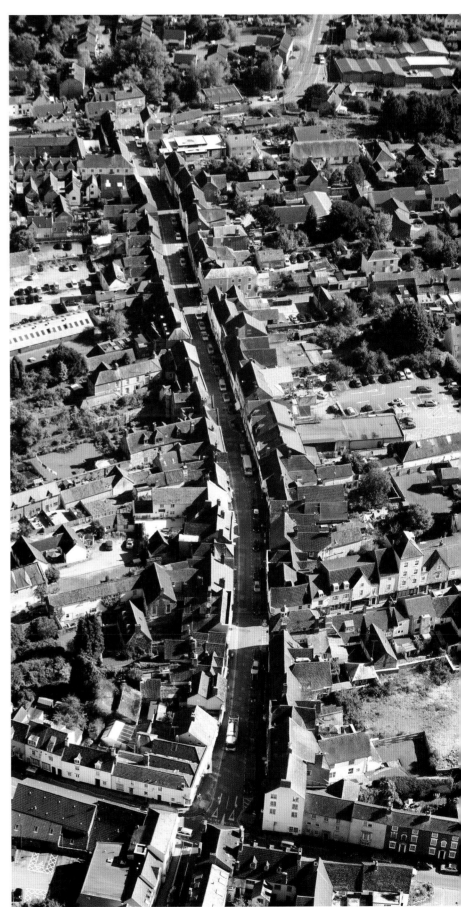

WICKWAR

Wickwar was on the Old Saltway and developed as a market town in the late 13th century. The wide high street reflects its function as a market and the fine parish Church of the Holy Trinity reflects its prosperity. It is of 12th century origin but it was extensively remodelled in the 14th and 15th centuries. Inside there is a sculpture of St John the Baptist dated 1496. The Old Rectory to the west of the church dates from 1864; it is an imposing house with an interesting crested doorway. A medieval-looking tower to the south of the town is in fact an airshaft for a railway tunnel.

NORTH NIBLEY

North Nibley is a small village between Wotton-under-Edge and Dursley. Above the village, on Nibley Knoll, stands the Tyndale monument. Tyndale was a prominent Protestant in the time of Henry VIII who produced the first complete translation of the New Testament in English. He was martyred in Vilvorde, Flanders in 1536. The 111ft high Tyndale Monument was built in 1866 using stone from Hampton Quarry, near Stroud. The tower can be climbed using an internal winding staircase and fine views are available from the upper platform. The parish church is largely Perpendicular in style but features an unusual 19th-century French-Gothic chancel.

KINGSWOOD

The village of Kingswood was formerly a detached part of Wiltshire that was incorporated into Gloucestershire by an Act of Parliament in 1844. Its current population is in the region of 1,290 people. A 16th-century gatehouse is all that remains of a former Cistercian abbey that was located on the north-east edge of the village. Founded in 1169 by William of Berkeley, the abbey's monks came from the Cistercian house at Tintern. The abbey was surrendered at Dissolution but its deeds are reputed to contain the oldest surviving Rent Rolls in England.

North Nibley monument can be seen at the top of the photograph, above, with the estuary of the river Severn. In the distance are the Forest of Dean and the Malvern Hills.

KINGSCOTE

Kingscote is in the high country near Dursley and features a 13th-century church. Amongst the interesting monuments in its churchyard is an unusual triangular stone pyramid. A tablet in the church announces that it was there that Catherine Kingscote married Edward Jenner, the discoverer of vaccination. Another famous village resident was John Wedgwood (1766-1844), the founder of the Royal Horticultural Society, who lived in the house known today as Kingscote Park. In the 1820s substantial Roman buildings were discovered at Kingscote and there are many other Roman sites nearby.

PART FIVE
EAST COTSWOLDS

Just as the western part of the Cotswolds is dominated by the river Severn and its tributaries, the eastern stretch of the uplands is dominated by the Thames and the rivers that flow into it before it makes its way to Oxford, London and eventually the sea. Like the rest of the Cotswolds many of the towns in this area owe their prosperity to wool but others developed because they lay on important trade routes; there are also a good number of communities that derived their wealth from the stone of the hills themselves. Many of the colleges in Oxford owe their distinctive warm colouring to Cotswold limestone and, thanks to transportation via the river Thames, Cotswold stone was a favoured material in the rebuilding of London after the great fire in the 17th century. St Paul's Cathedral is a particularly fine example of the use of Cotswold stone.

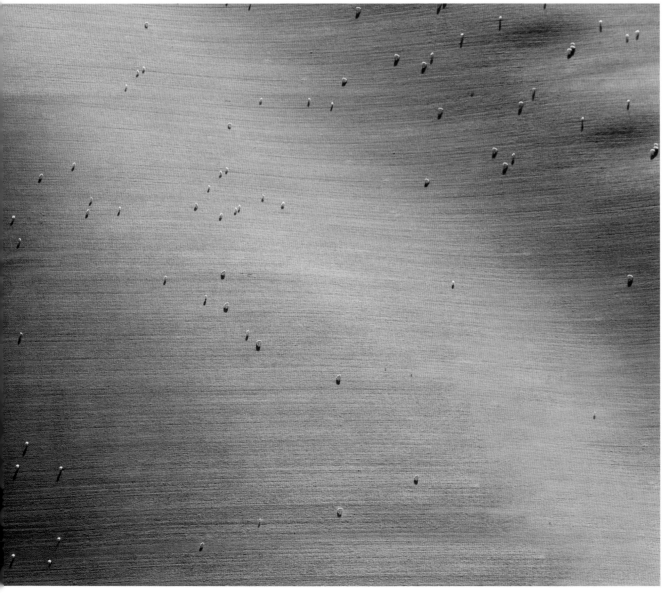

Sheep dot the rolling pastures (left) close to Shipton midway between Cheltenham and Northleach. Overlooking Lodge Park, Sherborne (above).

ROLLING HILLS

Although not very high by most standards the Cotswolds has many upland areas. The hills attract relief rain from the prevailing westerly winds and the limestone hills act as a natural reservoir. Many streams and rivers emerge in the Cotswolds before making their way down to either the Thames or the Severn valleys. As the rivers have travelled over the years they have carved out many delightful valleys some of which are steep but many of which are wide, sheltered and suitable for farming. The combination of relatively gentle hills and a plentiful water supply is yet another of the Cotswolds' attractions.

BURFORD

Regarded as the gateway to the Cotswolds, Burford built its reputation on wool, quarrying and coaching. Wool was important from the 14th century onwards and stone from quarries near the town graces some of Britain's finest buildings, ranging from Blenheim Palace to St Paul's Cathedral. Burford's heyday as a coaching town came in the 18th century when it was an important stop on routes into Oxford and London. Burford's steep and wide high street marks it out as both a transport and trading centre.

Amongst Burford's most interesting houses are the 17th-century Great House and a row of handsome almshouses which were built in 1457 and partially rebuilt in 1828. The church is interesting both architecturally and historically. The original Norman tower is surmounted by an elegant 15th-century spire and there is also a fine two-storey fan vaulted south porch. In the interior a memorial carving includes the first representation of Amazonian Indians in England and the font preserves the autograph of a Leveller prisoner who was kept in the church during the Civil War.

ASTHALL

The small village of Asthall nestles in the Windrush valley but its history has not been without incident. Nearby barrows suggest an Iron Age settlement and in Roman times Asthall was a staging post on Akeman Street, which linked Cirencester with St Albans. The church of St Nicholas dates back to the 12th century and features additions and alterations in a bewildering variety of styles. Asthall's Elizabethan manor house was home to the Mitford sisters and much of *Love in a Cold Climate* was written there. Its author, Nancy Mitford, is buried in the nearby Swinbrook churchyard.

MINSTER LOVELL

Minster Lovell is another village that combines an idyllic rural setting with buildings and ruins that reflect the village's interesting and varied past. A bridge across the Windrush leads to a high street that has a well balanced selection of thatched cottages and other Cotswold stone houses. St Kenelm's church was built in 1431 and has an attractive vaulted ceiling underneath the central tower. Some of the stained glass may be original and there is a fine alabaster knight's tomb, probably that of William the 7th Baron of Lovell who built the church and manor house; the house dates from 1435. Also worth noting is the round medieval dovecote.

LEAFIELD

Leafield is a largely unspoilt village
that lies between the towns of
Witney, Burford and Charlbury.
Near the centre of the village is a
barrow that, at 650ft above sea level,
used to be the highest point in
Oxfordshire, but this distinction
was lost after local government
reorganisation in 1974. The village
centres on the green which has a
school, founded in 1839, in its
middle. Leafield's most prominent
landmark is St Michael and All
Angels' church. Designed in 1859
by Sir George Gilbert Scott, its
distinctive spire helps walkers
to orientate themselves for many
miles around.

SWINBROOK

Swinbrook is another tiny village in the Windrush valley; it is approximately two miles east of Burford. North of the village is Swinbrook House which was built by David Freeman-Mitford, 2nd Baron Redesdale, and inhabited somewhat unhappily by his talented and beautiful daughters. The novelist Nancy and her sisters Unity, Diana and Pamela Mitford are buried in Swinford graveyard. The church dates from about 1200 and has an unusual open-sided bell-tower which was added in 1822. It is most famous for the 17th-century Fettiplace monuments which show members of the Fettiplace family reclining rather uncomfortably on various pieces of marble.

WIDFORD

The hamlet of Widford neighbours Swinbrook. It was a substantial village in medieval times but now few houses remain. Characteristic crop-marks of former buildings can be seen in the surrounding fields. The ancient church of St Oswald sits on a rise above the river and was built over a Roman tessellated pavement. The interior features a number of wall paintings dating from the mid 14th century. The one of St Christopher is badly defaced so that only his staff is clearly visible. There is a better preserved, and no doubt frightening at the time, painting of kings and ghosts to be seen in the chancel.

BARRINGTONS

Great Barrington began its life as an estate village and much of it remains so today. A great deal of the stone that makes the Cotswolds so distinctive was quarried in the area surrounding this village. Barrington Park was originally the seat of the Bray family but it became the property of Earl Talbot, Lord Chancellor in the reign of George II. The sloping, hollowed out village green in Little Barrington, above, is on the site of one of the quarries that supplied the Cotswolds with its distinctive stone. Respect for stone can be seen in the construction of some of the cottages which incorporate original medieval doorways into their structures. The village also produced one of the most famous stonemasons of the 17th century: Thomas Strong who worked with Sir Christopher Wren on St Paul's Cathedral and many other London churches. Little Barrington's own church is Norman in origin and has a number of distinctive features.

WINDRUSH

The village of Windrush is named after the river on which it stands and features a small tree-lined green next to an attractive church. It is a former quarrying village and possesses many fine houses built from the local stone. St Peter's church is of Norman origin; its south doorway is carved with menacing looking beaked heads. In the churchyard there is a finely decorated "wool bale" tomb, representing the source of the wealth of the deceased in the form of corded bales of wool. South of the village is the Iron Age hill fort of Windrush Camp, below, of which only the banks can be seen.

TAYNTON

Taynton stone, quarried nearby, was highly prized during the middle ages and early modern period and can be found in local buildings, Oxford colleges and many of Sir Christopher Wren's London churches. Stone from the Taynton quarries would have been hauled overland to the Thames for transport by barge. One account describes a load of stone being pulled by a team of 21 horses.

Taynton church dates from 1450 and is unusual in being in the Decorated style rather than Perpendicular. It features some excellent stone carving: the font has an octagonal bowl with kneeling angels at each corner and figures of beasts, Evangelists and a mermaid in between. There are also vividly carved corbel heads in the nave and north transept.

LITTLE RISSINGTON

The RAF aerodrome at Little Rissington achieved fame in the Second World War and maintained it through its association with the RAF Central Flying School and the Red Arrows air display team. The station was opened in 1938 and closed in 1994; it is now home to a volunteer gliding squadron. The Norman parish church of St Peter's at Little Rissington contains a stained-glass memorial to the men who lost their lives in the service of their country and the graveyard contains several rows of their graves in simple Portland stone.

FAWLER

The river Evenlode flows through its wide and fertile valley as it makes it way from its source near Moreton-in-Marsh to its meeting with the river Thames at King's Lock about three miles north of Oxford. Fawler is a typical hamlet on the river's banks benefitting from the river as a water source and, in earlier times, a means of power and transport. The Fawler Mill House was built in 1660 and is a grade II listed building. There are traces of a Roman villa at Oatlands Farm.

ASCOTT-UNDER-WYCHWOOD

Settlement at Ascott-under-Wychwood, indicated by a hill fort and a long barrow, goes back at least to the Iron Age. In Norman times a motte and bailey castle dominated the area but little of this remains. As can be seen from the photograph on the right, its site is largely occupied by Manor Farm. In 1873 sixteen Ascott-under-Wychwood women were arrested and imprisoned for trying to prevent strike-breaking. Riots followed in Chipping Norton and eventually Queen Victoria issued a royal pardon. The women are known as the Ascott Martyrs. In 1874 at least four of the women and their families emigrated to New Zealand where they now have many descendants.

SHIPTON-UNDER-WYCHWOOD

The village of Shipton-under-Wychwood, left, centres on its church and village green. The church tower is 13th century and the interior features a 15th-century stone pulpit and font and a Tudor wall monument. The Shaven Crown Hotel, which overlooks the green, was formerly a monastic guesthouse and is thought to be one of the 10 oldest public houses in the country having been a hostelry for 700 years. William Langland, the author of *Piers Plowman*, was a tenant in Shipton-under-Wychwood and John Foxe, the author of *The Book of Martyrs*, was a minister at the church.

CHARLBURY

The large and prosperous village of Charlbury is mentioned in The Domesday Book as belonging to Eynsham Abbey. In 1256 it became a market town; evidence for this is revealed by the wide Church Street which gives access to the parish church of St Mary. The church has Norman origins but has been extensively remodelled so that it now has elements in Decorated Gothic, Perpendicular Gothic, Perpendicular and Gothic Revival styles. Lee Place, the former Dower House of Ditchley, and currently the summer home of the Duke of Marlborough, occupies a small park on the outskirts. Charlbury used to be a centre of glove-making, but the trade died out in the 1960s.

SHERBORNE

Sherborne is an estate village that served the nearby Sherborne House. Many of its buildings are now owned by the National Trust. The first house here was built between 1651 and 1653 for a Mr John Dutton but the current building, in a 19th-century Renaissance style, dates from the 1830s. The Dutton family occupied the house until 1940 and there are many memorials to them in the adjacent church of St Mary Magdalene. This dates largely from the 19th century but retains part of a 14th-century tower. Sherborne House has now been divided into privately-owned apartments.

CORNBURY PARK

The Cornbury Park estate contains around 1,700 acres of the Wychwood, the most ancient woodland in Britain. The earliest building at the park was a royal hunting lodge. In 1642 the property was given to the Earl of Danby and the south wing of Cornbury Park dates from this period. There have been numerous other additions in the intervening years, amongst them the country's first ha-ha: a sunken wall that kept deer out but allowed an uninterrupted view. Nowadays Cornbury Park is developing a reputation as a venue for a summer music festival.

BOURTON-ON-THE-WATER

The five ornamental bridges spanning the river Windrush in Bourton-on-the-Water give it a unique appeal and the nickname of the Venice of the Cotswolds. Bourton-on-the-Water is served by the parish church of St Lawrence. The only visible part of the old church is the chancel, built in 1328 by Walter de Burhton. In 1784 the Norman church was largely replaced with today's neo-Classical style building with its thick tower housing a clock and bells. Further additions were made in the 1870s when the present nave was constructed. The nave roof is a fine example of a king-post roof. On the edge of the village are a series of flooded quarries which have been established as a nature reserve and contain varied collections of birdlife.

QUENINGTON

The village of Quenington, below, lies on the banks of the river Coln; it contains some excellent 17th-century houses but is chiefly noted for the church of St Swithin. This features two 12th-century Norman doorways; the south doorway shows Christ crowning the Virgin Mary and the north doorway strikingly illustrates the harrowing of Hell. In recent years the village has become known for its biennial Fresh Air festival of sculpture. This take place in the five-acre garden of Quenington Old Rectory and gives visitors a chance to see and interact with modern sculpture in an open-air setting.

EASTLEACH MARTIN AND EASTLEACH TURVILLE

Eastleach Martin and Eastleach Turville are two villages that face each other across the river Leach. Each village has its own manor house and its own church. Eastleach Martin has the larger of the churches and its 14th-century north transept is graced with three Decorated-style windows. Eastleach Turville's church has a 14th-century saddleback tower and a Norman tympanum. The two churches are 200 yards apart and the villages are connected by two bridges. One bridge carries the road but the other, "Keble's bridge" is an unusual construction of large flat stones; it commemorates the Keble family who were lords of the manor of Eastleach Turville in the 16th century.

FAIRFORD AIR BASE

RAF Fairford is the home of the Royal International Air Tattoo, an annual air display which is one of the largest in the world. It is also the place where Concorde made its maiden flights. The base was constructed in 1944 as a facility for British and American airborne elements of the D-Day landings. During the Cold War Fairford became a base for divisions of the USAF Strategic Air Command and a 10,000ft (3000m) runway was constructed in 1953. The base last saw active service during the 2003 Iraq war and is now on standby status, but it is capable of being re-activated within 48 hours.

HATHEROP

Hatherop is bracketed by two fine country houses; the village adjoins the parkland of Williamstrip, a 17th-century country house that was the seat of Michael Hicks Beach, the first Earl St Aldwyn, and the village itself contains Hatherop Castle. Parts of this building date back to the 16th century but it was partly rebuilt for Baron de Mauley in 1850-56 by the architect Henry Clutton. Clutton also rebuilt the church of St Nicholas at around the same time. In 1867 Sir Thomas Bazely acquired the house and spent some £200,000 on improving the estate and planting 380 acres of trees. Hatherop Castle is now an independent co-educational preparatory school.

LECHLADE

Lechlade grew up as a market town in the early 13th century. It profited from the Cotswold wool trade but its main source of wealth was as a staging post for goods and passengers. Cheese was an important cargo in the 17th century and, after the Thames and Severn canal opened, coal became important. With the development of the railways in the 19th century Lechlade became an appealing destination for boating and fishing enthusiasts. In spite of the meandering of the Thames in this part of its course Lechlade remains popular with narrowboats and other leisurecraft. At the centre of the town is the church of St Lawrence, which dates from 1476. Not far from Lechlade is Kelmscott Manor, William Morris's summer home which is now an arts and craft museum.

AROUND STROUD

The long history of human settlement in the Cotswolds has left many marks on the landscape. Iron age forts were often sited on hills for ease of defence, Roman roads carved the area up with straight lines to facilitate military transport and the growth of sheep farming in the middle ages led to the opening up of large unitary fields. Later still canals, railways and modern roads provided new routes through the region. Probably the most characteristic boundary marker in the Cotswolds is the drystone wall. Built with great skill without any binding materials these massive dividers criss-cross the Cotswolds as a permanent reminder of the efforts of countless nameless shepherds.

BORDERING THE SEVERN VALLEY

Stroud (above) and Dursley (right) both lie on the Cotswold Way which follows the ridge of the long escarpment and looks down over the Severn Valley to the west.

STROUD

Five valleys come together at Stroud making it a natural centre for trade and transport. In the middle ages Stroud quickly established itself as a centre of the cloth industry and at the height of its prosperity there were around 150 cloth mills in and around the town. Stroud was particularly famous for manufacturing the cloth used in military uniforms. The centre of Stroud reflects its role as a market town with its many narrow streets and its Tudor town hall. The area known as The Shambles catered for butchers and the 19th-century neo-Classical Subscription Rooms provided entertainment. The exuberant neo-Gothic School of Science and Art reflects the community's regard for education.

The decline of the Cotswold wool trade did not dampen Stroud's spirits over much and the area increasingly became a centre for light industry in the late 19th and early 20th centuries. Even today there is a small textile industry in the town; for example, the green baize cloth used to cover snooker tables is made in Stroud. Happily the growth of industry did not seriously diminish the town's charm and modern Stroud emphasises its relaxed atmosphere and alternative lifestyles. The town now plays host to lively music and dance festivals and to a flourishing arts scene. Pavement cafes and small art galleries are common. A prizewinning farmers' market, launched by Jasper Conran and Isabella Blow in 1999, takes place on a regular basis and independent food shops have returned to the ancient Shambles. The five valleys that meet at Stroud provide easy access to different parts of the Cotswolds and so make the town a good starting point for visitors.

LYPIATT PARK

Parts of Lypiatt Park date from the 14th century. In 1395 Richard Whittington, Lord Mayor of London, acquired the manor and by the Tudor period it had been extensively remodelled. Unfortunately in 1645 the house was burnt down by Royalist troops in order to expel its defenders. In the mid 19th-century a neo-Tudor style range was added and further Gothic Revival alterations were made in 1876-77. By 1959 the house had fallen into disrepair, but the sculptor Lynn Chadwick purchased it and worked on its restoration until his death in 2003. Since then there have been plans to open part of the park to the public to create a permanent home for Chadwick's sculpture collection.

RODBOROUGH

The village of Rodborough is on the edge of Stroud and occupies the end of a spur of land which rises to over 600ft. Rodborough church has a stained-glass window depicting Thomas The Tank Engine in memory of the Rev Wilbert Awdry who lived in the village from 1965 onwards; the village is also the home of Winstones Cotswolds Ice Cream. Above the village is Rodborough Common; the ancient road from London to Stroud used to run across here and provided the village with carriage trade. The Bear of Rodborough is a well-preserved white-walled coaching inn built during the 18th century.

117

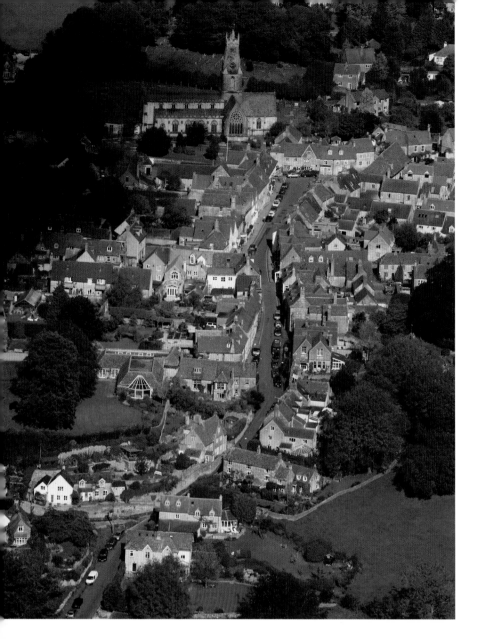

MINCHINHAMPTON

The 600-acre Minchinhampton Common was granted to the people of the village in the 16th century; to encourage the settlement of skilled people any weaver was allowed to enclose land on it and build a cottage. The common is now owned and managed by the National Trust and its elevated location makes it a popular destination for ramblers. The town square features a war memorial and a 17th-century market house and still plays host to a market every Thursday. The high street is an eclectic mix of building styles from different eras with a highlight being the 18th-century Crown Hotel. In 1863 the spire of the parish church of the Holy Trinity had to be demolished for safety reasons. It was replaced by the current rather unusual "coronet". The church also has a 14th-century south transept and some interesting brasses.

AMBERLEY

Amberley is located on the western edge of Minchinhampton Common and commands splendid views over the steep Avon valley. Amberley is a scattered settlement that has taken various guises over the centuries. The original woodlands in the area gave way to sheep-farming during the middle ages. Most of the older buildings in the area are former weavers' cottages. The parish church at Amberley was not built until 1837. As well as being a popular recreation area the common contains several important archaeological sites. The most visible and extensive Iron Age remains slightly pre-date the Roman conquest and indicate that the site was a strategic location for the *Dobunni* tribe. Known as the Minchinhampton Bulwarks these large defensive earthworks are over a mile long. Nearby is Amberley Camp which is a hill fort enclosing around 50 acres. There are also many round and long barrows in the area.

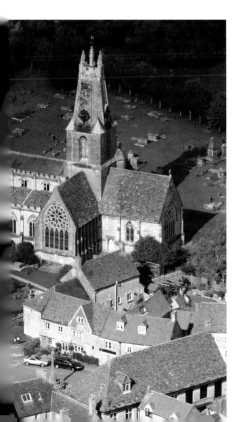

NAILSWORTH

Nailsworth is at the meeting place of three valleys which branch off towards Avening, Horsley and Stroud. Access to the village was probably quite difficult in the middle ages and would mainly have been via packhorse. The village's plentiful water supply enabled the construction of large woollen mills and one of them, Egypt Mill, has now been restored with its waterwheels and most of its gearing still intact. The building operates as a restaurant. The nearby Ruskin Mill has become an arts and crafts centre and also has a working waterwheel. At the centre of the town there is a fine mid 20th-century clocktower and many of the steep and narrow streets contain substantial buildings from earlier periods; one of the most notable is the fine 17th-century Quaker Meeting House.

DURSLEY

Dursley is on the edge of the Cotswold escarpment where it descends into the Severn Vale. It sits on the river Cam and is surrounded by attractive walking country; the Cotswold Way passes through. Dursley developed as a market town in the 13th and 14th centuries. The Church of St James the Great dates from the 13th century, but the surviving structure is mainly from the 14th and 15th centuries. Its original spire collapsed in 1699, killing some bell-ringers; it was replaced by the current tower in 1708-09. A pillared market house featuring a statue of Queen Anne and a bell turret dates from 1738. A recent rather dubious distinction for the town is that JK Rowling, who was born nearby, named Harry Potter's odious stepfamily after Dursley.

HORSLEY

Horsley village developed around the crossroads to the east of its 12th-century church. The crossroads were probably also the location of a market. The medieval church was rebuilt except for its tower in 1839. The four-storey tower dates from the 15th century. A house of correction built according to the principles of the reformer Sir George Onesiphorous Paul was opened in 1791 on the site of a medieval priory but it was closed in 1878. On the edge of the village is the Ruskin Mill College; this is centred on a former fulling-mill and provides education for students with learning difficulties in the traditional economic activities of the Cotswolds: textiles, weaving, farming and forestry are currently studied.

ULEY

Uley sits in a wooded valley of the Cotswold escarpment. In the early years of the industrial revolution the village was renowned for producing blue cloth. The Gothic Revival Church of St Giles situated near the village green dates from the 19th century and was designed by Samuel Sanders Teulon; it replaced an earlier Norman church. The village was once famous for its large number of pubs (around 14) but there is only one there nowadays. Alcohol still features in the local economy, however, in the form of Uley Brewery. The modern brewery, set up in the 1980s, operates from the site of the Price Brewery in buildings that date back to 1833. Water for brewing is provided by a natural spring on the site.

OWLPEN

The Owlpen Manor estate includes the manor itself, a 19th-century church, a small 18th-century mill and a number of cottages nearby. With an adult population of around 35 the parish of Owlpen is the smallest in Gloucestershire. The manor house dates from 1450 to 1616 and it was extensively restored in 1926 after almost a hundred years of neglect and dereliction. It features a Tudor great hall, a Jacobean solar, an early Georgian little parlour and a great chamber. The latter room contains unique painted cloth wall-hangings showing Biblical scenes from the life of Joseph and his brothers. Owlpen Manor is reputedly haunted by Margaret of Anjou, the queen consort of Henry VI.

WOODCHESTER

Woodchester is on the western slopes of
the Avon valley and is divided into North
and South Woodchester by a smaller
valley. The parish Church of St Mary's
was designed by Samuel Sanders Teulon
in Gothic Revival style; only the early
Norman chancel arch and part of the
north wall survive from the original
church. Another notable building is
an unusual double round house which
would originally have been used for
grain storage. Outside the village are
Woodchester Park which contains the
ruins of a large 19th-century mansion and
Woodchester Roman Villa which features
the Orpheus mosaic, the second largest
of its kind in Europe.

BISLEY

The many fine houses in and around Bisley are a testament to the wealth created by the cloth trade in the 18th century. At one end of the village are five water chutes known locally as "the Wells"; they were restored as wells to commemorate the Rev Thomas Keble, brother of John, who was rector of Bisley for nearly 50 years. The graceful church spire towers over the local landscape and dates from the 13th-century. As was common in many Cotswolds communities the village has a small 19th-century two person lock-up; with its ogee-gables Bisley's is a particularly fine example. At the top of the high street the Stirrup Cup public house dates from the mid 19th century.

PAINSWICK

The stream below Painswick once provided power for its woollen mills whilst the purity of its water made the village an important centre for cloth dyeing. Many of the houses in the village date from the 17th and 18th centuries and once belonged to wealthy wool merchants. At the centre of the village is a fine church which combines sections from the 15th century with an elegant 17th-century tower. Surrounding the church are well-tended colonnades of yew trees which have been in place since 1792. Local legend has it that there are only 99 trees as the devil always kills the hundredth. Painswick Bowling Green is over 400 years old and is still in use.

COWLEY

The most striking feature of this village, which sits in the Churn Valley between Cheltenham and Cirencester, is Cowley Manor. The original Cowley Manor house was built in 1695 but it was replaced by the current Italianate house in 1855. This was then extensively re-modelled 40 years later for Sir James Horlick of the famous Malted Milk Company. Cowley Manor is now a luxury hotel. The gardens contain several natural springs and have many water features; an upper lake feeds a cascade and the lower lakes are part of the river Churn. The 55 acre site is grade II listed. The local parish Church of St Mary lies next to Cowley Manor and dates from the 12th century.